FROM

QWAQWA

TO

EUROPE

———{-_-}———

It's the stuff that dreams are made of,

It's the reason we are alive.

SEKONYELA E. MOLEFE

GOD GAVE ME MY BOOK.

GOD GAVE ME MY BOOK.

Contents

****

Sekonyela E. Molefe

Preface

———

I decided to write a book, mainly because I felt I had a story to tell about my life. With my background, many people in the same shoes as mine tend to take different routes that lead to destruction. Many in better shoes than mine tend to waste their advantage, and allow those like myself to catch up with them and even pass them on the way.

****

My efforts will yield fruits in due time. When someone is heading in the wrong direction, those watching can see. It's the same as when someone is in the right direction. It's those kinds of efforts many do not realize, even in their own lives besides mine. We have achieved so much in our lives, but we tend not to consider our achievements, because to us, man's success is money.

Sekonyela E. Molefe

I have written my story based on true-life events, and in the hopes of motivating & encouraging anyone who opens and reads this book, now and in the future, to reach for the stars and beyond. I have written my story to add to the many people that have come into this world and said: "in this world, you can be anything and everything you want to be."

****

Acknowledgements

———

To everyone who has impacted positively on my life, I wish to take this moment to thank you. May the Lord continuously grant you knowledge and wisdom to impact on the lives of people you come across in this journey of life.

Thank you.

****

****

I greet you in the name of our Lord and Saviour, Jesus Christ of Nazareth.

****

CHAPTER ONE

———

MY NAME IS.

My name is Sekonyela Eric Molefe. I come from humble beginnings indeed. I was born on the 19th of March in the year of our Lord 1990. My mother says I was born at the Elizabeth Ross Hospital in QwaQwa, South Africa. When I was born, my family lived in the village of King Nchabeng, where my father's family is based to this day.

****

My mother met my father while she was working in a sewing factory, and my father was an ambulance driver. My mother and father moved from the villages to a township called Club View. At that time, my father was working as a truck driver delivering water to many places around QwaQwa which did not have water, and my mother was working as a cleaner at an old-age home and people with an intellectual disability centre.

I remember my life starting from Club View. I started school in crèche at Riverside and from crèche, I attended elementary at Tataisong where I did my Grade 1.

I remember while in Tataisong, we used to be given food which I did not like, and that really made the teachers cross with me. My class teacher would always shout at me for not eating and finishing my food, and once she threw her shoe at me for trying to hide the food I did not eat. I took my plate that still had phuthu pap and milk, put it in the middle of a stack of plates and put other plates on top, and it made a mess.

****

I made it through Tataisong, and I remember my Tataisong Grade R graduation day which was at Thiboloha School for the Deaf and Blind. I sat next to my cousin and his friend. We were all in Grade R, but they were in another class and another building, so I did not really know them that well. I remember I wanted to cry, or I cried a little because I could not see my mother, but my cousin and his friend calmed me down by saying to me: "Why are you crying? What are the girls going to say? Look, here are girls, talk to the girls and stop crying. You are going to see your mother after graduation." And I stopped crying. I felt the boys were smarter.

After my Tataisong graduation, I moved to Letlotlo Primary School.

****

Letlotlo primary school was my home for the next eight years of my life. I failed two grades there, grade three and five. I moved to Bloemfontein during grade six to stay with my mother who had since separated from my father. After three months, I moved back to QwaQwa to stay with my father. During my time in Letlotlo, we moved from Club View to a two-room shack in Phuthaditjhaba. My parents got divorced, and my grandmother died in the year 2001.

I cried.

From Letlotlo, I moved to Mafube Intermediate School with an impressive report.

****

Mafube Intermediate School

I stayed in Mafube Intermediate School for the next three years under the leadership of Principal Dlamini. During grade seven, I was not serious with my studies. I played a lot during that time. My mind was all over, but by the grace of God, I managed to pass that grade.

In grade eight, my friend passed away. I was asked to speak as a friend during his funeral service, and when my time came to speak during the funeral service, instead of speaking, I cried. I was overwhelmed with grief and unable to speak, but I said: "rest in peace, my friend."

In grade nine, I was asked to read during class, and I was unable to read. I remember in grade nine me and some of my friends tried to cheat during a Sesotho test, and we were caught and kicked out of class. I am still afraid of cheating to this day. In grade nine, my mother made me an appointment to visit the doctor for a circumcision at a private surgery.

****

I prayed to the Lord that he would help me know how to read. I practiced how to read and write, and the Lord made a way. During grade nine, I played soccer and excelled. I became the leading scorer for the school's soccer team with many goals to my name. During those days, I made many friends, and in those years many young people started being wild.

At that time, young people could have decided to be young and responsible people, but because of the pressures of the societies we live in, life and its many obstacles, challenges, opportunities, life being life, life being unpredictable and the will that happens not being ours, but being God's will, many young people lost their way. They began to be lost, and the sad part is that they did not even realize it.

****

It is sad that many young people from the ages of 14 to 18 lose their steps. They trip and fall into the snare of the devil and forget God Almighty who has been with them since the beginning. They forget the Almighty who has been with them every step of the way, and they begin to mature/ grow up, get accustomed to the systems of this world, to the ways of doing things of this world.

Young people started to enjoy sinning. They could see what money can do, and they now had opinions of their own. Young people now love, and like certain things and want certain things for themselves. Young people choose what is important to them at that moment, and most of them make wrong decisions because they are young and not knowing, and they do not have proper guidance from the elders. Not to say the elders do not guide the young and do everything in their power to guide, protect, love and show young people the right path. They do, but at that time, young people are stubborn, and they think they know what is right for them. Now all of a sudden, we know more than our mothers and fathers, sisters, and brothers.

****

The church needs to step up strongly at this time and lead the children to the light which is God. Even at church, the devil follows the children because he knows they are a threat, and he wants to destroy them at an early age. Kill it before it grows. Many children grow up in the house of the Lord. Many people that I know did, and they fell during the way.

They fell of course because of the devil that attacked and deceived them, but they need to be strong and know the ways and tricks of the devil. During those days of Mafube intermediate, when our characters were beginning to shape. One of the organisations that gave us information was Love Life, and only a few people went willingly, and it taught us some of the important lessons about life. For example, out of 100 in my school, about maybe 15 attended, and the remaining rest learned about life from other sources, wrong people, wrong ways, from people who do not have knowledge, and that is why many get lost. We learn from people who are away from God, and people who do things according to the standards of this world. We learn from people who are lost, and people who have accepted to live their lives in darkness.

Few people learn what's right, and they stand a better chance of succeeding in life. Wow! Life is unpredictable and nobody knows what tomorrow holds, but the Alpha and Omega.

****

We need to invite God almighty into our lives, give our lives to him, and live for him from an early age.

Our lives will be better, our futures will be brighter and better than our grandfathers, grandmothers, our mothers and fathers, because that is where we get it wrong.

Yes, we need education, but most importantly, we need Jesus Christ even more. We need Jesus Christ to help us understand the knowledge we get in our schools, and to be able to denounce the wrong knowledge we may come across during our lives. We need to be able to stand up for ourselves and do what is right in the eyes of the Lord, instead of swimming and drowning in sin, generation after generation.

We can defeat many evils that make us go astray, the devil does not have power.

****

CHAPTER TWO

———

I HAVE MANY SCHOOLING YEARS

High school

In high school I told myself I was going to be more outspoken, outgoing, performing, and engaging in school activities and in the class. I must admit. I almost thought that meant being a menace, but because the Lord is always with me, he did not lead me to that way, but led me the right way.

****

In high school I found myself. In high school, I met travel, tourism, and hospitality studies. I had an option to choose between accounting studies, science, computer studies and tourism studies.

****

One of my teachers advised me to go for accounting studies, but I had a problem with math from previous years. I have a saying that: "if I had gone for math subjects, I might have not finished school," because I struggled with that subject, and tourism studies had less difficult math. That choice I made took me to places, taught me so much and showed me the world.

I really wanted to perform at school with my studies. I pushed myself. I met many people, and I did many things.

I went to Johannesburg for the first time at age 15 with the Shona Khona soccer competition.

Grade 12 in 2009 is the year I remember the most in my basic education schooling career. I started smoking marijuana, and a year earlier I had started with cigarettes. I chose the girl I liked and went after her. I became the head boy at school. I finished school at 19 years.

****

I chose to study further. I wanted to study, and that did not cross my family's mind. I had to tell them about going to university, and the Lord made a way. My grandmother who works as a teacher said I had to go to university to further my studies, and she wanted me to go to Cape Peninsula University. Of my mother's three children, I became the first to go to university.

I wanted to go study in Durban after our grade 12 school career exhibition trip which was held at the Greyville Racecourse in Durban, KwaZulu-Natal. I loved Durban and the ocean. It was my first time there, but my family advised me to go to Bloemfontien as my brother and sister where there working.

****

I learnt in grade 12 that life begins after high school. After high school, you have to push yourself and go after what you want. There are no more schoolteachers forcing you to do your homework. Now you deal with professors and lecturers who give you work, and you have to do it yourself. You do as you want. If you want to do it, you will do it. If you don't want to do it, you don't do it, and you fail. The choice is yours.

All the knowledge we gain during our school years is important as it is preparing us for the real world. Nevertheless, we are young and we take it lightly. Life.

****

CHAPTER THREE

JIMMY GOES TO JOBURG

AND

ERIC GOES TO BLOEMFONTEIN

The saying Jimmy goes to Joburg can just be changed to Eric goes to Bloem.

The world is big, trust me the world is big outside of your comfort zone. Church pastors call it the real world. The world outside of the church and praying with the people who believe in the same thing as what you believe in. There are many more people with many more ideas, beliefs, and ways of doing things. That is the real world.

In the real world, it is very easy to fall, very easy to trip and fall, very easy to get lost. It is very easy to get lost, that is why you need Christ on your side more than ever to be your light and path giver, and to protect you at all times. The relationship with Christ will save you from many things of this world. Psalm 91 says it.

Feel it, it is here.

Feel it, it is here. The year the 2010 soccer world cup was playing in South Africa. That was my first year at university, at the Central University of Technology. That was my home for the next six years of my life. I was studying a course that takes two years and six months. I did my diploma in six years.

My first year at university was an eye-opener for me, I failed. I failed pretty much everything. I played, big city lights got in my eyes. I did not know what I was doing, and why I was doing it. No one from my family had ever been to university. I had no one with prior knowledge as to how I should be and what I should do in university. My sister and brother helped me a lot, and others did not have anybody around. We are faced with different challenges in life, and we deal with them in different ways. Everybody you see in this world is faced with something, something that if you were in that person's shoes you wouldn't know what to do, but we are all pushing forward and giving it all we have at all times. Others give up.

****

If you think what you are going through or your situation or problem is hard, if you can only hear what the person next to you is going through. For what you are going through, you will say thank you Lord and appreciate your life more and what you have. The Lord sees us all and hears us all.

A young man from the villages in a big city.

But I fought, but my fight was not enough, I lost. I must say as I was faced with challenges, and what was happening in my life, others understood what was going on, they were focused, they understood what was happening and what they had to do and what they must not do. They understood what is important for them and what is not. They also fought, and they won. It was easy for some. They were well-prepared, had help, had what it takes, but it also needed effort from their side.

Others are under really hard conditions, no food, no accommodation and even resort to prostitution/ crime for money. Some are in situations our human minds do not even think are possible, but others are going through them in their lives and at university and despite all that, they make it still.

There are many realities we are unaware of, and when they are revealed to us our whole lives and the way we see the world changes forever. The creator of the heavens and earth loves all of us. They all did well, we all did well. The way it happened is exactly the way God planned for it to happen, even before the earth was created.

****

I had challenges in my life. Luckily, and I say luckily for lack of a better word. Whether it was by luck or on purpose only God knows. But I found Jesus Christ. The very same Jesus Christ who I was given by my family as a little boy, but lost because I was also lost like many people are before they find the right path. I too enjoyed the things of this world.

After failing my first year I wanted to drop out of university. I was given advice that I was not the first person to fail. I was advised that I needed to go back with a different attitude and mindset, and I did exactly that. The Lord also gave me strength to fight. I fought, and I won.

****

Life's challenges were there, many, many, many of them and as many as they were, Jesus Christ was by my side all the time.

Now that I look back, I realize that I was nothing without Jesus Christ, and even now in the present. I am nothing without Jesus Christ, and even my family's future generations are nothing without Jesus Christ.

The best advice in the world is to follow Jesus Christ, and the best finding in the world is to find Jesus Christ.

When we have Jesus Christ on our side, we have the creator of the heavens and earth. He who created all and who everything belongs to. Everything.

****

CHAPTER FOUR

———

"YOU LOOK LIKE A HOBO, STREET KID, A JUNKY"

My time after university. As others were going up, I was going down. I lost myself drinking, smoking, waking up and sleeping without doing anything productive. I had lost hope on life. In life, there are ups and there are downs. I was down and I did not even know it. My mother told me, my sister told me, people said I look like a hobo, a street kid, and a junky. I was too high to realize.

One day, one of my university friends passed by my house on his way to Durban from Bloemfontein. When he saw me, he could not believe his eyes. He told me that I was not like that even when I was at university away from home. He said I am at home and living with my mother, and I am the way I am. He said I needed to find a job, any job that would keep me busy and give me a reason to wake up in the morning. I was down and it took me time to realize I was down and not up.

I went back to Bloemfontein and got a job. I worked at the Windmill Casino for about three to four months. That time too while in Bloemfontein, I had money but did not see what I was doing with it. Unlike during my days in university when I had little money, now I was working and earning a salary but misused the money. I went deeper into the dark. I left the casino when my grandfather passed away, and I did not return. My Grandfather became my close friend towards his last days. We spoke about many things, even this book you are reading.

I wanted it from him and he did not write. I told him I would write. He accepted Jesus Christ as his Lord and Saviour. I asked him some difficult questions. We cried together, he was close to his last days and mine were just beginning. He told me how hard life can be. He told me about his youth and upbringing. I enjoyed visiting him. My grandfather passed on at the age of 92. He loved his cows.

****

I went back to QwaQwa, and while in QwaQwa I got a job as a trainee at a Game Store in the warehouse department. I worked there for about two or three months.

Later, I left that job. I felt that job was not the one I wanted, it required physical strength. I always told myself that I wanted to work with a paper and pen, and on the computer, because I grew up thinking that our forefathers sold themselves as strong and having strength, and I was not going that route with my life. I worked hard to be educated, and still wanted to get more education. I have always seen myself as a person with brains and not physical strength. Even my children must know they have brains and are capable of building the greatest cities of this world, run the financial systems of this world, the political spectrums of this world, they too can be kings and queens in this world. I am the only person I know who is black and grew up in the townships who would say out loud that I want to own banks, and my peers would look at me like I am out of my mind.

****

My mind never told me that I can only work for the greatest corporations in this world, but I can own them. When meeting new people, others would say: "that might be my boss, so I have to behave right," and I would say: "I need to monitor that person to see if they could qualify to be my employee."

****

I am someone who always told the guys when talking and googling the highest-paid soccer players in the world and their salaries, that I don't want to know about those people, but I understand that they are paid, and the person that I need to be looking for and learning from is the person who pays them. We all have different ways of looking at the world. People think and believe that certain things cannot be achieved or done, but I believe that with man, many things are impossible, but with God, it is possible and not with me. I am under the Lord's hand and his will is the one that happens and not mine, so it is not for me to say what is possible and what is not possible, what can be achieved and what cannot be achieved.

I was taught at home that what matters is life, and as long as we are alive, we can achieve anything and everything we want.

Leaving that job at Game Store also taught me that you don't leave what you have before you get something else to replace it with, because now, I was unemployed again. To put bread on the table is better to do what you are doing as you are looking for something else, but different people do things differently. Like for instance, take musicians as an example. Musicians will not look for work to do, and they will decide to work on their music because they believe that is what they are called for, and they won't do anything else besides music. No problem with that, but who then is going to put bread on the table before the music starts making you money?

Again, the job did not kill me, but it made me stronger, and in retail, there are vacancies that come out for one to apply for. Many people from around the world work in retail. I always say yet again, I was under the influence of marijuana, so my thoughts were not right at the time.

There are so many things I wanted to do that required money, but where was the money going to come from? I did not know.

****

I am sharing some of the decisions I made while smoking marijuana, and at some point, I even thought of doing illegal stuff, making and selling drugs. That one is very easy to take, many take it unaware of the world it is putting them in, unaware of the repercussions of their actions and how that trade is going to affect their whole life, that decision changes the way you view the world and people.

****

Time went, and my sister took me to driving school and gave me her old car in hopes that I would change my life around and find my way. I did not finish driving school, so my father took the car because I was driving without a driver's license. I remained unemployed.

Sekonyela E. Molefe

During that time of my life reality hit me. I did a lot of thinking. I realized that it had been years my mother complaining about me smoking marijuana. For all those years, I did not feel or hear a thing that she was saying, but it hit me that what I was doing was hurting my mother and my family, and I had to stop. During that time, I decided to stop smoking marijuana, and I did. I remember the moment I stopped like it was yesterday. It was at night. I had rolled a joint at my home as usual, my mother was in the house, and I was standing outside like I normally did while smoking. I lit the joint and during the smoking, after about three or four puffs. I told myself that this is the last joint of marijuana I am smoking and I will not do this again after I finish this one. As the joint I was smoking was about halfway, another thought came to my mind, it is not like I enjoy doing this, it's not like it is good for me, doing it hurts my family, it takes me to places I wouldn't go if I was sober. I labour for this thing. It makes me meet people I would have never met, it has even put me in trouble with the law. I must not be caught with this thing, so I am always on the run and fearing not to come across the police with marijuana on me. This thing does not do any good for me and my life.

I asked myself why I am even waiting for this one to finish. I immediately turned it off, walked to the drainage at my house and threw it in there, and even the one that was remaining in the bag. I opened the tap. Water came out, and I closed the tap and went back in the house. After that moment, I have never smoked marijuana again ever since that time. It was not easy, but after eight long years of smoking marijuana, I finally stopped.

****

For the first weeks and months without smoking, without doing something I had been doing for the past eight years about five days a week for eight years, sometimes for weeks and weeks without skipping a single day. I have gone for months without skipping a day. It was very new and very different, but I wanted to stop. I was tempted to smoke, but the Lord Jesus Christ helped me and I did not do it. It wasn't easy to stop, and the best advice is to never begin, never to start with drugs in the first place. Not even once. I was a heavy smoker of cigarettes and marijuana.

CHAPTER FIVE

———

TOURISM BUDDIES

Tourism buddies programme, Free State, South Africa. About three months after deciding to stop smoking marijuana, I started the tourism buddies programme in 2016. I had been unemployed for some time. In the tourism buddies, we attended classes at Tshiya Education Resource Centre and our practical work we did at the Golden Gate National park. It was my second time working at the National park. I worked there during my Central University of Technology diploma practical work. I met many new people during that time, and I even started a marketing course at the local college Maluti VFET Main Campus, and that made the number of new people I knew increase. I studied the marketing course for about two to three months and dropped out and continued with tourism buddies.

****

The most important part of that journey was that I became closer to the Lord. I took a step towards Christ and to this day, I do not regret. With only one step towards Jesus Christ and confessing that he is my Lord and Saviour, who died for my sins, and confessing that with him I am protected. Now I know that I can stand before the Throne of God with my path being Christ. Now I know that with me something's are impossible, but I can do all things through Christ who strengthens me. Yes, I can do all things through Christ who strengthens me. My life changed for the better.

****

I learned certain lessons and certain realities about life. One of the many is that, you never lose any battle or fight until you stop fighting. I also realized that one has to work to provide for their family and loved once. No one chooses the family they are born into, whether rich or poor. Rich or poor, we are all given a life by God to live it to the fullest according to his ways and standards. One can be born rich to die poor, and one can be born poor to die wealthy. It is up to you what you make of your life.

Like a bird in your hand, its life is in your hands, and whether the bird lives or dies, you are the one who will decide. When the ball is in your court, you can choose to throw it away, choose not to play and give it your all, or you can choose to play and give it your best effort to score and win. The world is your oyster. Yes, Life is an oyster and it's up to you how you open it. One can throw it away and see it as only being a shell, and one can slightly crush it with a rock and enjoy its contents. One can buy an oyster opener, open it and enjoy it. There are many ways of killing a cat. Working in the tourism industry presented me with a new and unexpected opportunity of a lifetime.

****

CHAPTER SIX

MOTHER, I AM GOING TO PORTUGAL

My mother was cleaning her house when I came with news of me going to further my studies abroad.

My mother did not even know where Portugal was located. She asked me which part of South Africa that was. She did not think it was overseas, but I explained to her that it is in another country and in another continent which is called Europe. We were both happy. My family and friends were also happy with me.

****

I am an African

I was born in Africa. I grew up in Africa. I played in the dusty fields of Africa. Be proud Africa, look at what you have done, look at your products. You've done great and continue to do more. You raised me and many more. You taught us everything we know.

We are your products, young and old, us and our mothers and fathers, even our forefathers.

With all the struggles, and challenges we face on a daily basis. All the knowledge we have and all the knowledge we lack.

You have your own Africa. Those who talk African, who walk African, who are shaped by Africa and are originals from Africa. Some say unique from even the way they walk. I guess it's the winds, the dust, the rains, the sunshine and the hard surfaces of your land we walk. The kinds of food you feed us. It's what you make us, it's how you want us to be, different from the others. Our obstacles and differences are what put us together, and what separates us. All those and more make us who we are and give us our unique identity. You are great Africa. One can go as far as to say you are the greatest of them all. You are greater Africa, greater than them all combined.

****

CHAPTER SEVEN

———

AFRICA

Africa, you give our lives meaning. Millions and millions of people spend their whole lives only knowing you. They never get the opportunity to get out and go to other continents, but they live their full lives and make the most out of them only knowing you, our beloved home. You qualify to be the world on your own. You deserve a wall around you to be protected, even people from outside of you once they come to you, they never want to leave. We the living hear people from places such as Asia which are lands far, far away say with their own mouths: "I want to die in Africa." I don't even want to touch on our European brothers and sisters, they love you so much they named your streets after themselves. They say Cape of Good Hope was their first contact with you in South Africa, and they've loved you ever since. I know you, I know your splendours and wonders, who of the living wouldn't love you? Your beauty is majestic, you are attractive to those who have eyes.

There are other places on earth with oceans and mountains, blue skies and rains, winds and peaceful tranquillity, but there is none like you Africa. You are in a league of your own, like heaven on earth. You've given, you continue to give, and you will continue to give. Anyone who wants to get from you has to come to you. If they had never come to you, to this day, they wouldn't have known all about you.

****

Good-bye Africa

When I left my mother, that's when it started to sink in my head that I am leaving QwaQwa and South Africa. When I entered my father's car, I was very sad and felt like crying, but my father asked what was wrong. My father said to me that I should be proud. He told me to go and make a future that I want for myself. He said none of my family members has ever been to Europe, and none has ever even thought of going to Europe to study for three years, and he said that I should grab the opportunity with both hands, work hard and make my family and myself proud. At that moment, I stopped missing home.

****

For many times while I was away from home people kept on asking if I do not miss home, and my reply was always: "No, I miss my family of course, but I do not miss home. I am on a mission and I won't miss home up until I am finished with it." What I was doing, I was doing for the little ones in my family. I was doing it for them to see as they grow up that the world is big, and our survival is in Christ Jesus. I was doing it for my family's future generations, the Molefe children.

While I was in Bloemfontein, I was high on marijuana and drunk on alcohol, a combination of the two. Now I have more experience, but I still need more education. For as long as one is alive, one will always learn, each and every day of their existence. People such as Nigerians, Ghanaians, Arabs, Europeans, Americans and Asians pride themselves with their education and chasing after education. They go to all sorts and kind of heights, running and chasing after education. Wherever it is, they will go after it, and they will get it. They will work hard and do whatever it takes to have it.

****

While I was at the Central University of Technology about to finish my diploma, I felt like I had acquired all the knowledge in the world at that time, but little did I know that it was only the beginning. With all the knowledge in the world, having little knowledge or no knowledge is not good for humanity. People need education. Africa needs education.

At the Central University of Technology, I read a saying that said, one has acquired a diploma and has reached and achieved their goal in life, and now begins a lifetime of learning. Learning is a life-long journey for the living, as long as we are alive, every day of our lives we learn. It is a lifetime of learning here on earth. The bible says: "the beginning of knowledge is the fear of the Lord." Knowledge is good, and that is good knowledge, but there is also bad knowledge. Both are knowledge. We need to ask the Lord to show and reveal to us good knowledge and hide us from the bad knowledge, for us not to see it, hear it or speak it with our mouths. The bible says: "the Lord will show you good knowledge, things you do not know, hidden things, and even things you didn't know exist."

CHAPTER EIGHT

EUROPE

Europe is not Africa

In Europe, there's advancement, it's peaceful, clean, the people are knowledgeable, law-abiding citizens, lovely people and beautiful and classy women. Overall, I felt like there is a place like this in Africa, in South Africa. There is a part of Africa that is like Europe, even if it's not the Africa I come from and grew up in. Only because I come from a part of Africa that is considered rural, with African problems such as unemployment, illiteracy, crime, wars, lack of housing, low education, corruption, lack of healthcare and many more problems classified as African Problems. Not the whole of Africa is like that, that is why I say some parts of Africa are like Europe. Truly speaking, I felt it in my heart that as beautiful as Europe is and many more wonderful things I mentioned. The fact is that there are places in Africa that are the same as Europe.

****

There are places in South Africa that I believe are or might even be better than Europe in their own right. They may be small, but Africa has them, such as Clifton in Cape Town, George, Summerset West, Houghton, Sandton, Plettenberg Bay and many more that can go tit-for-tat with the best cities the world has to offer, and we are only in South Africa only talking about South Africa. What about Pharaoh's Egypt, what about Somalia, what about Angola, Ethiopia, Tanzania, Seychelles, and many more African countries?

****

There are places in South Africa where you can spend your whole life not knowing you are in Africa. You can be sure that you are in Europe or America.

You can fly and sail anywhere in the world you want, and instead of going to your house in Malibu, Monte Carlo or Marbella in Spain, you go to South Africa with your private jet or your yacht. You'll get what you can get when you are anywhere around the world, you will find wonderful places in South Africa that you can find anywhere else in the world.

****

Europe is ahead with knowledge, capital, technology, education and more things that put one ahead of others, but there are still people just like in South Africa, those who have jobs and those who don't, those who are educated and those who are not. They also have crime, all sorts of crimes, cybercrime, white-collar crime, hijackings, pickpocketing, bank robberies etc. They also have corruption in the government, private sector and industries like all over the world. Like anywhere in the world, only a few people live the luxurious lifestyle, and like anywhere in the world you still need to work to have money. It is the same as anywhere else, and the money you work to have is only for survival and not a luxurious lifestyle. If people can make it in South Africa and become billionaires, I can also make it in South Africa and become a billionaire. If people can make it in America, in Europe, In Australia. If someone can become a billionaire in China, among people who are close to two billion, what is stopping me?

****

If one can become a billionaire in India, among a population of over a billion people, what is stopping me because I even have an advantage which is the Lord Jesus Christ on my side? He who created the heavens and the earth, and he who the silver and gold belong to. One of the richest men to ever live by the name of John D Rockefeller said in one of his books: "God gave me my gold," and from that, I pick up that he had gold, and he understood that it came from God. Our lives are not in our hands at the end of the day. It is God's will that happens, only his plans come true, that is why we need to come close to him every time. We need to come close to God so that he can reveal to us the secrets of life, and what we must do to survive and possess his silver, gold and all his riches while we are alive in this world, because the silver and gold belong to him, and we are going to leave it here on earth when we die.

Naked we came and naked we shall leave.

Leaving all the riches we found here on earth, here on earth. From the soil we were made and to the soil, we return.

****

CHAPTER NINE

MADEIRA, JOU LEKKER DING

When I first arrived at the Island of Madeira, I said to myself here 80% of the population is knowledgeable, here the people can read, write, calculate and all they have to do is to teach the remaining 20% of the population. Even if it's not 80%, but there are more people who are literate than those who are illiterate. In numbers, it can be 70%, 60% or even 50%. Unlike in Africa where you find that there are more illiterate people, few people get formal education. You find 10% or 20% having to teach the remaining 80% which is an uphill task. Imagine 10% having to teach 90%, that is why they say only one percent of the world has all the wealth of the world.

I lived on the island of Madeira and it is wonderful, Madeira jou lekker ding.

****

I still feel like Madeira is like a province in South Africa. It is like a certain part of South Africa. Everywhere you go in the world, there is a part of South Africa, rural or uptown. That is why we are called "A world in one country."

****

CHAPTER TEN

THE GIRL I MET

The girl I met at Parkveg Police Station. She would say: "there is hope in the world." I have met many females/ girls, but the girl I met at Parkveg had a different view of the world. Her upbringing made her, it made her strong and an intelligent woman. Her life lessons and the way she held/holds herself is different from others, from other women I've met. I have not met all the women in the world, but I met the girl at Parkveg, and she is worth talking about and sharing to others. I called her my Angel. I felt the Lord had sent me an angel at a time in my life when I needed an angel. And an angel she was to me. She came into my life to show me a different way of life, a way I did not grow up knowing. I appreciate and still appreciate. The lessons came thick and fast, every day and every night, for the period the Lord had set. I give her credit for saying to me while we were in Portugal, come to service/ Church on Sunday where we meet and share about the Lord Jesus Christ.

In South Africa, I had already started, but during the time I arrived in Madeira, I had stopped because I had felt a church should be formal with a priest and congregation, but we were far from home, and the only church we could have was to meet with my fellow South African brothers and sisters and share about the Lord's word and praise and worship together. The Lord sent me an angel to make me aware that even if we are away from home, we can still meet and share about Christ unlike sitting and doing nothing, we meet and sing, praise and pray and share the word of the Lord. Life happened and the lessons came.

****

As I say, I have met many women/ females/ girls in my life. Sometimes I sit and wonder what impact I had on their lives, because without a doubt, they had many impacts on my life.

I pray to the Lord that he puts them under the shadow of his wings.

Memories.☺

CHAPTER ELEVEN

———

THE STRENGTH OF A WOMAN

The strength of a woman, my mother is a woman. You know whether we like it or not, one thing does lead to another. Positive thinking and positive living lead to positive ideas and right ways of doing things and living, and to the right situations and thoughts as well. Christ lived a sinless life and if we live life like that, we will get all the things he promised us. If he said he will do it, he will do it. Just like bad living and wrong living also lead to more negative and bad people and situations, troubles and a sinful life. They lead to DESTRUCTION. It is true that soft drugs lead to hard drugs. Beer leads to whiskey and brandy, and cigarettes lead to marijuana, and marijuana to mandrax and mandrax to meth/tik, and tik to heroin and heroin to crack and crack to cocaine. One thing leads to another.

****

Being among young strong women during the time when life was revealing its realities to me made me aware of what women go through

and how strong they are, and it taught me about the challenges they face on a daily basis in their lives, individually.

The kind of strength women have can only come from God himself. Women on a daily basis are faced with temptations of this world, making decisions, dealing with friends and loved ones, dealing with men, money, life, family, education, and many more things which I cannot mention in one book. But the fact of the matter is that women go through a lot in life. It's not easy being a woman. The strength they have comes from God.

In other parts of the world, women are not even allowed an education, they can't drive or hold any significant position or role in society. Their place is in the kitchen, and they are only considered good for making and taking care of babies.

****

Women are seen as objects that men sleep with, they take care of the house, even all that which is given to them to do, they do it exceptionally well, but it is not acknowledged or considered as work. It's work that somebody must do, but when women do it, it is not considered as work. We as men forget that if the women did not do that work/ job, nobody would do it. It would be a whole that needs to be filled. Women fill it, but nobody notices.

A woman can be proposed by 50 men at every corner she takes. 50 corners, 50 men with 50 different proposals/ presentations, as to why she should pick or go for him, or why he is better than the last guy or the next guy. Oh! Do you think a Ferrari is nice? The next guy at the next corner comes with five Ferraris, a Bugatti and a mansion. For one person, having to say no to all those presentations and proposals is hard, knowing many women's backgrounds, coming from nothing and saying no to a guy that drives a Ferrari and offers her money is hard. Even men wouldn't be able to say no to that. That's what women are faced with on a daily basis.

****

Also, some women think they can't make it on their own. They think they need help from someone else. They doubt their abilities, and that results in them settling for less and being treated like trash by the men. The society we live in is distorted.

Women are not aware of the strength they have, and what the Lord has given them. The strength of a woman can only be possessed by a woman, and us men can only imitate the strength that women have. The strength of a woman is not about sex, beauty and their body, but it is what makes any woman and every woman a woman. All women have it, they only have to find it in them. Many women think the strength of a woman is being able to take care of a man's needs, his children and his house, but that is wrong, that is just a drop in the ocean of what they are capable of. There's more than what meets the eye in women, way more, rulers and queens of this world.

****

Women who are with their families through thick and thin, that is the strength of a woman given by God that keeps them going. Women that fail need to know that they are not the first to fail and failing does not mean the end of the world. Many people have failed before, it became difficult for you. You have passed other things, you are not worthless or useless, there are other many more things that the Lord has made you good and perfect at, and

you pass them all the time. Just because you fail in others does not mean you are a failure. Both men and women.

Women don't have to sell themselves short and say that is how the Lord made them, those thoughts come from the devil. We all fail here on earth. When we tried walking as babies, we fell and failed. When we tried speaking, we wanted to say mama but said momo. It is difficult for everybody on earth. Women have it difficult of course, but women give in very easy. Women tend to like easy things. Things given without effort put in. Women hold economies of countries, but women do not understand. Women sing "girls run the world," but they do not believe it.

****

The devil is a liar. He lied to them and continues to lie to many more women so that they never find their true strength and potential. Have you ever asked yourself why the snake did not tempt Adam but tempted Eve in the bible? A man wouldn't stand a talking snake, but a woman knows anything, and everything is possible in this world. What is a talking snake to creation? The devil roars like a lion waiting for someone he may devour. The Lord who is the creator of the heavens and the earth knows the present, the past and the future.

God made women for a reason. Women are strong and women do wonders.

****

At the age of 28, the Lord opened my eyes to see the strength that women have. In the bible in the Book of Genesis, it says the Lord opened Hagar's eyes to see a well of water. She was not blind, but the Lord opened her eyes to see what she could not see, and it was right before her eyes all along, but she did not see it until the Lord revealed it to her.

That is why many people still need to be made aware of what women go through and what they are capable of, and maybe the mindsets of men towards women will change. I never understood why men treat women badly and call them names, aren't all our mothers women? You can hear a man refer to all women and call them names, but you will hear him say my mother is an exception. We need to learn to respect women, even before we have daughters for children, because many men don't respect women but want their daughters to be respected. What a paradox. The solution is to respect all women from the start.

I would say men have been disrespectful towards women since a long time ago, and men being taught to respect women won't change anything, but in this world, things change and I believe this too shall change, nothing remains the same forever.

Men that respect women are seen as stupid, come to think of it even women who are respected by men feel those men are weak.

****

They have gotten so used to being mistreated, talk about the children of Israel not wanting to leave Egypt because they thought slavery is a way of life for them. Our sisters are used to being mistreated, which is wrong. In my long life, I have learned that even the earth is a woman because it has the power to reproduce, it's Mother Nature. How do we treat it? We are faced with global warming, and we face many natural catastrophes caused by our actions, which are the result of us treating earth bad. Things need to change: our mindsets about women need to change.

I looked at the women in South Africa, famous and not known women. I looked at women around the world. I looked at women who I grew up in their eyes, from my school teachers to women around the streets and

community that I grew up in, and I noticed their strength, perseverance, dedication, love, knowledge, wisdom, their struggles, hardships, challenges, problems, and solutions. Take a look at what women go through and face on a daily basis in their lives, individually and as women in general as a whole.

I started speaking highly of women making men and women alike aware of what women are capable of. I even included it in my book as a piece of knowledge worth sharing. I started speaking highly of women of South Africa, speaking of women such as Mama Albertina Sisulu. Women who opened my eyes through my own personal research, women such as Oprah Winfrey, Mama Winnie Nomzamo Madikizela Mandela, Folorunsho Alakija of Nigeria, The Queen of England, Her Majesty Queen Elizabeth II, the female President of Liberia, Ellen Johnson Sirleaf, female President of Brazil, Dilma Rousseff, female President of South Korea, Park Geun-hye, female President of Croatia, Kolinda Grabar-Kitarovic, former African Union Chair Dr Nkosazana Dlamini-Zuma, Felicia Mabuza-Suttle, Maria Mother of Jesus, Sarah, Hagar and many more powerful women. How can I

forget our great grandmother, grandmother Eve?

I set out on a mission for myself to learn about the women of South Africa, about women from Africa, Europe, Asia to America and Australia, and the rest of the world. What great knowledge did I come across. It's the Lord who led my every step and thought.

I noticed that like the earth is there on a permanent basis, women are also there on a permanent basis. You can't ignore them, shield them, hide them, or rule them. Women are part and parcel of life. The world is what it is today because of the contribution of women. Earth wouldn't be the same earth we know if it wasn't for women. Who knows what it would have been like if it were men alone on earth, the guys would have probably killed each other, and left the animal kingdom on its own with the vegetation to rule over themselves.

Women are our equals before the Lord, they start from scratch, and they achieve their goals. They learn, and they educate, they are loved, and they love, the world has leaders,

and they are leaders too, who can lead at any given time and place when given the chance. They give birth and bring life on earth. They bring life to all the people on earth and in the world. My view on women had totally changed as old as I am. I know women deserve equality, respect, to be honoured, to be loved, understood and considered.

Sekonyela E. Molefe

Take counsel, women are a force to be reckoned. Ignore them, and ignore and leave out God's marvellous creation, God's knowledge, God's might.

****

CHAPTER TWELVE

———

MEN

Men are not steel that does not feel pain.

****

Like women, men are also God's marvellous creation.

****

CHAPTER THIRTEEN

———————

YOU NEED TO LEARN TO HAVE SOUND REASONING

My reasoning scares me. I have always been an explainer. I have always explained, spoke on other people's behalf to the point of being asked if I was people's lawyer. At that time, it didn't bother me, I was probably high. Lying was also part of the explaining, you feel you are a good talker, and you add a few lies and things go your way, and you go forward. Lying was not my thing, I have always read books, watch documentaries and researched, so that gave me an upper hand in my explaining because it provided me with more information. I am one who knows there is good knowledge and bad knowledge, and when you have either of the two, you have knowledge and that is the bottom line. I never had to lie, I had too many facts and knowledge to pass around and make genuine conversation and teach and be taught in the process.

****

I discovered later in life that people who lie are compensating for lack of knowledge. For example, if you know how to cook, you know how to cook, but if you don't, you will say you know how to cook knowing very well you can't. You lie to compensate for the knowledge you lack. If you had the knowledge, you wouldn't have to lie, but you lie because you don't have it. You lie because you can't do it. You know it can be done, but you lack that knowledge of doing it.

That's why Satan operates with lies, he lies because he knows if people knew the truth, they wouldn't go with him. It will change the situation, so he lies and deceive people so that they follow him. With the truth, he would stand for opposing God, and the people wouldn't follow him, so he lies so that he can have followers.

One of the reasons I stopped smoking cannabis was my explanations. They would be so elaborate and so accurate, but along the way I would drift from what I was talking about to something else. I would think of something else which emphasized what I am talking about, and I would end up not finishing what I was talking about and forget what I was talking about altogether.

In my conversations, explanations, and teachings, some people would pick up that drifting and leaving conversations in the middle, and would say to me: "you speak so well, you explain well but the problem is that you leave conversations and explanations in the middle, and move on to something else and start talking about another thing before finishing that one you were talking about."

So, I guess what I was saying, ended up not making any sense. Of course, I was high and drunk. what do you expect?

Now realizing that I may be good, I thought to myself, is it that I am so talkative when drunk and or/ when high, or I am like that naturally? I thought to myself, if God wanted me to be like the way I am when drunk and high on marijuana, he would have made me to be born like that. If I am a talkative person whom when reasoning people keep quiet and listen to what I have to say, then I must do it sober and not under any influence of any substance.

I stopped smoking weed first, because I did it on a daily basis, in time came cigarettes and finally, I stopped drinking alcohol. All of them, I stopped doing permanently.

At first, I kind of felt like I was different but soon realized that I am exactly the way God wanted me to be without any influences of any kind of substance.

Now that I am sober I can even get work done. I am happy with the way I am. All those things were distractions in my life. I am glad and I thank the Lord, that I was able to get rid of them in my life. I know how hard it is for others who still go to them on a daily basis, but deep down, they want to stop. Many people say it out loud that they want to stop, but they can't or say they are not ready.

People ask me all the time how I was able to stop. The people that know I was a heavy smoker and drinker are left amazed when they hear I no longer engage in those things knowing the level I was doing them with, and while they consider themselves as doing them less than me, but finding it difficult to stop. That is why I don't hide it and say I received help from the Lord, by myself, I was never going to stop. We take our time and go to them, they don't come to us, we keep on returning to them. We need to ask the Lord to help us get rid of those evils because they do not bring good in our lives.

CHAPTER FOURTEEN

———

THE KNOWLEDGE OF GOOD AND BAD

Bad is very easy to do and fun to do.

Good requires patience, good is not easy, it is painful.

Given the choice to choose between the two, mankind will take the first and justify his actions by giving many earthly reasons as to why they do the bad. Many people are doing bad every single day. One can go as far as saying the world is doing bad because it is easy and not challenging, and there's no pain involved, but it is killing us, and we live to please the devil and not the Almighty who is the creator of the heavens and earth. Look at the history of the world and look at how many bad things have been done. At some point, it was so bad the creator had to end the world. It got so bad the creator had to send His only-begotten Son to die for our sins.

****

Talking about life

Talking about life and its ups, and downs. Talking about the rich and the poor, the educated, and the not educated, the whites, blacks, Asia's and Jews, the systems that run the world, politics, religion, science and all the things included in this life. I call them the things that make life what it is. When speaking and sharing and expressing my opinion which like everybody else I am also entitled to. Many say it's like I speak for the rich, but I explain and ask if they would rather I speak for the poor. Capitalism rules and runs the world we are in, it has been like that for many centuries and continues to be like that. One could swear that is how life is supposed to be.

Why pretend it's the poor who make all the decisions because we all know it's the rich. And that is the reality.

****

I have always liked talking. I have a saying that people I have met in my life at some point in their lives make reference to the things I have said or say something they heard me say. They base whatever they are saying on the knowledge, piece of advice or wisdom they got from me.

I sometimes told many people I have met while growing up, that when you have grown and have children, tell your children about me at least once. I made people aware of many realities of life and its ups and downs, about how the rich behave and live, and about the poor. I made them aware of who has what and how it helps them advance in life, whether it is big or small.

****

I made many people aware of the systems, and people that rule the world. The mediums of communication that can rule and do rule the world. About politics and governments, taxation and how the world runs.

Many would say I speak for the rich, but you have to look at the world from the point of view and perspective of the rich. They make all the decisions not the poor. They look to see if they are going to benefit first, and they consider the poor after. That is the reality. If the rich are going to benefit, the poor can die. They don't care. If they are alive, that's all that matters.

Knowledge from God

The beginning of knowledge is the fear of the Lord.

I ask for knowledge from God. I seek Him first and more shall follow. Sometimes I wonder what others think of me when they hear me speak, again there is a saying that says: "keep quiet and people do not know how you think, and speak and show everyone how stupid you are."

Brothers and sisters, we are continuously fighting the devil and his many temptations, every day and every night of our lives.

He tempts us every day. We have temptations continuously, and we must call on the Lord Jesus Christ to fight the devil on our behalf because we don't have the strength to fight Satan. The battle is the Lord's. He is the one who can fight Satan, that is why God sent his only-begotten Son to die for our sins and defeat the devil for us.

****

Never think with your human flash you can fight the devil. He will crush and annihilate you on sight, and not that I am glorifying Satan, but only Jesus Christ and through Jesus Christ, we can defeat the devil. We fight the devil with Christ Jesus.

****

Satan has a fishing rod in his hand that has bait specifically for you. Every single day of your life when you wake up, he is already flashing something in your eyes, putting thoughts in your head, offering you many of his temptations for you to take and so that he can have his hook on you. If the day goes and he sees you have not fallen for what he offered you in the morning when you woke up, he does not stop, but he changes what he was offering to something else, If you don't take it, he puts money, he puts alcohol, he puts partying, he puts crime, he puts drugs, he puts lies, girls/ boys, cheating, stealing, all kinds of temptations are being thrown at you every minute of your life by the devil. He does not stop, he is always after you. That is why the bible says we must pray all the time, never cease to pray, pray continuously. The bible says we must not stop praying. The bible says we must pray all the time.

The bible is God's word, and God says we must pray all the time because the Lord our God who created the heavens and the earth, the moon and the sun, the stars, and the air

we breathe, knows very well that the devil is always looking for someone to destroy.

Invite the Lord in everything that you do in your life. I invite the Lord Jesus Christ in everything I do in my life.

While I was writing this part of the book, I was on the book of Jeremiah in the Bible, having started the Bible from Genesis in the beginning. In the book of the Prophet Isaiah, the Prophet says without knowing, unexpectedly you can get the shock of your life, without knowing anything, and at that time, the Lord had already knew and known that, that is going to happen. He is the Alpha and Omega, the beginning and the end. He is the present, the future and the past. Glory be to the Lord Almighty God.

****

CHAPTER NOTE

WHY I WROTE THIS BOOK

The reasons I wrote this book

1. The book will entice many people's minds and brains to learn new knowledge they do not know.
2. The book will act and be a motivation for people to be aware that with God the creator of the heavens and earth you can do and get many things you never thought you can get. What is impossible with man is possible with God.
3. The book will encourage many people to read.
4. The book will educate people and make them more aware of the world we live in.
5. The book will encourage people to talk more and express themselves more. Discuss what is written in the book, argue, disagree and agree and engage in conversations.

6. The book will help people know that it is possible to get rid of the negative influences in our lives, and still continue living our lives perfectly.

7. I have always wanted/ prayed to the Lord to have a product of my own, such as a sauce, cell phone, beans, spice or soup or anything that belongs to me that comes from my mind from start to finish. This book, my book, is that product which I have always prayed for and have always wanted. The Lord answers our prayers all the time in many ways. The Lord gave me my book.

****

****

DEEP

I have given my life to Christ Jesus, and I love it.

The deeper I go, the more Pastors and Teachers I come across. The more wisdom and knowledge comes to my life. The Lord keeps on giving.

In too deep, and I love it.

It is a whole new world for me. People get into the world of drugs and alcohol, and the crime world too. There are many worlds. The Lord, the creator of the heavens and earth showed me the door/ way to Christ's world, and for that, I sing and I shout, for Jesus came down and he lifted me up. I thank God.

Amen.

****

****

Life is going on

****

Sekonyela E. Molefe

Product of Sem Co. Holdings

P.O BOX 16279
WITSIESHOEK
9870
PHUTHADITJHABA
QWAQWA

EMAIL: FQQ2EUROPE@YAHOO.COM

FACEBOOK: ERIC MOLEFE
TWITTER: @ERIC MOLEFE SE
INSTAGRAM: @ERIC MOLEFE SE

****

Sekonyela E. Molefe